A SEA FULL OF SHARKS

Written by Betsy Maestro

Illustrated by Giulio Maestro

SCHOLASTIC INC.
New York   Toronto   London   Auckland   Sydney

ISBN 0-590-43101-3

21 20 19 18 17 16 15   8 9/9
                    Printed in the U.S.A.   09

Thinking about sharks can make you shiver with excitement. That's because sharks are truly awesome creatures. When something is awesome, you feel respect, fear, and wonder all at the same time. Most of us feel this way about sharks — a little scared, but very curious.

Tiger Shark

Sharks have been around much longer than people.
They have lived on earth for about 400 million years.
But we still do not know that much about them.

A fossil
shark's tooth
from millions
of years ago
(actual size)

A tooth from
a great white
shark of today
(actual size)

A sharkproof cage

Because live sharks are so hard to study, even scientists still have a lot to learn. They do know that there are 350 different kinds of sharks. Scientists have grouped these into 30 large families. Sharks in the same family are very much like each other.

There are more different sizes and shapes of sharks than you would imagine. Some are huge creatures as long as 50 feet (over 15 meters), while other sharks are tiny and may be only 6 inches long (15 centimeters)! Most sharks, though, are about 6 or 7 feet long (1.8–2.1 meters).

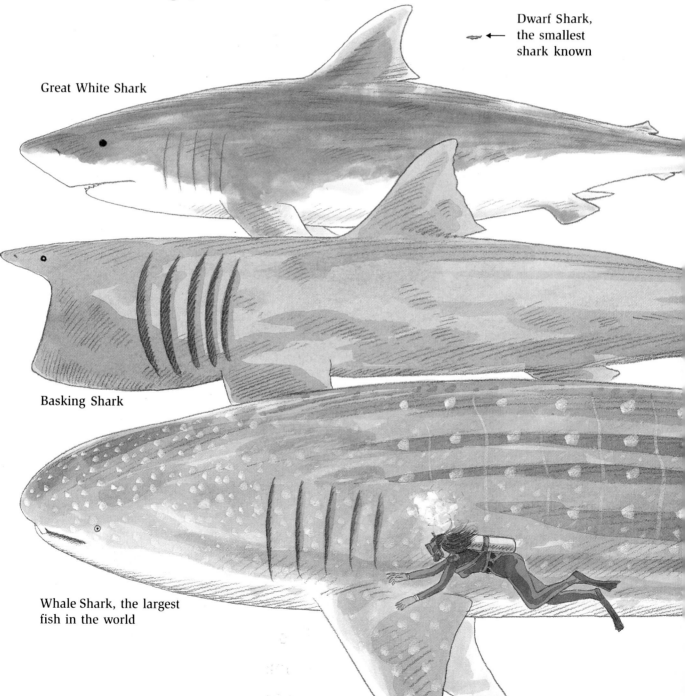

Dwarf Shark, the smallest shark known

Great White Shark

Basking Shark

Whale Shark, the largest fish in the world

With 350 different kinds of sharks, it is easy to understand why they do not all look alike. The body shape, tail shape, and teeth of sharks differ greatly from one family to another.

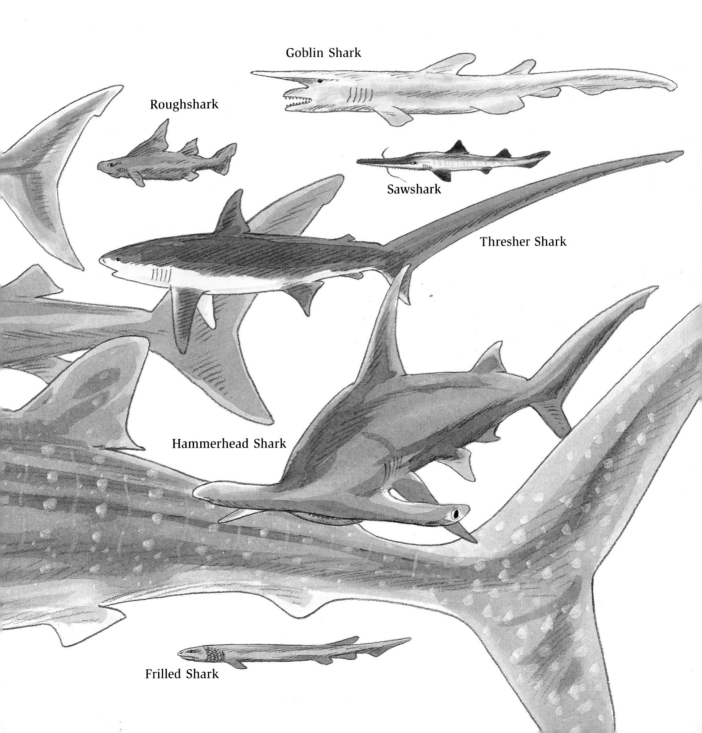

Goblin Shark

Roughshark

Sawshark

Thresher Shark

Hammerhead Shark

Frilled Shark

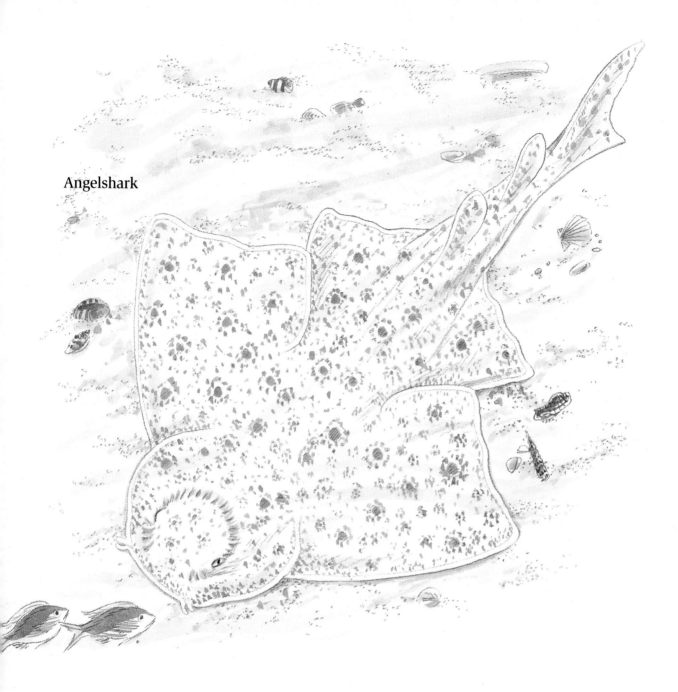

Angelshark

Just as all sharks do not look alike, all sharks do not live or act in the same way. Some sharks live at the very bottom of the sea, hardly moving at all. They bury themselves in the sand and wait for their food to come to them.

Other sharks are very active, swimming great distances in the deepest ocean waters. These sharks can swim at speeds of about 40 miles per hour (64.4 kilometers per hour) looking for their food. Some may travel all over the world during their lives.

Requiem Shark

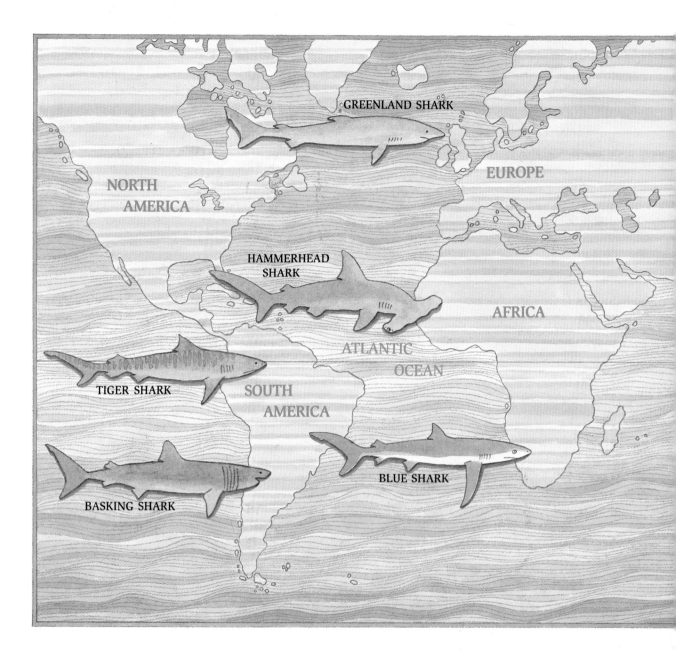

Sharks live in all the waters of the world. Certain kinds of sharks stay in certain kinds of water. Hammerheads, tiger, and bull sharks usually like the warm waters of tropical places.

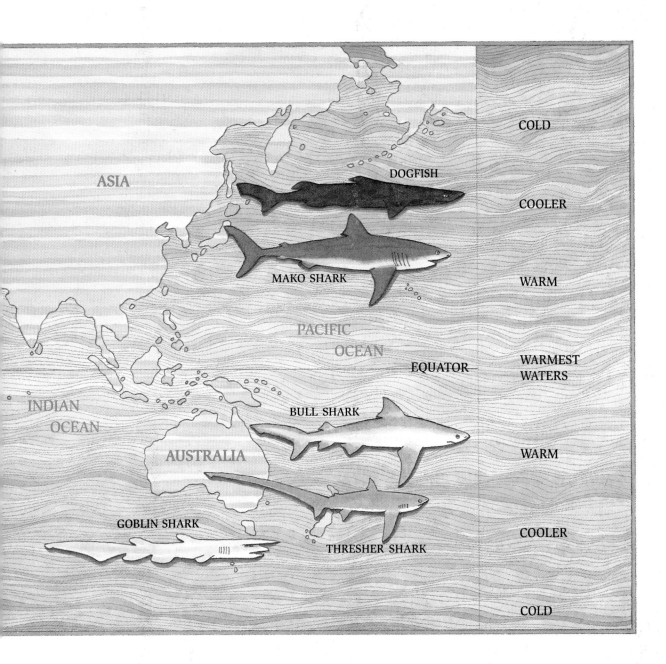

Sharks such as the thresher, basking, mako, and blue prefer water that is neither too warm nor too cold. They live in the mild waters, not too far north or south. Other sharks such as the Greenland, dogfish, and goblin swim mostly in colder waters.

Only about 25 kinds of sharks have been known to actually attack people. Most of the dangerous sharks are large, and usually eat big fish and mammals.

Great White Shark

A person swimming in the water may look like a tasty meal to a shark. The great white, tiger, bull, blue, and hammerhead sharks are all known to be very dangerous to people.

Of the remaining 325 kinds of sharks, most are smaller animals and not normally harmful to humans. Some are actually rather gentle creatures, interested only in eating small plants and fish. The whale shark, though huge, is not dangerous.

It swims slowly through the water trapping tiny animals and plants in its mouth. Divers can sometimes hitch a ride on its fins. Basking and nurse sharks are included in this group of more or less harmless sharks. But any shark, if disturbed or angered, could bite and injure a person.

Whale Shark

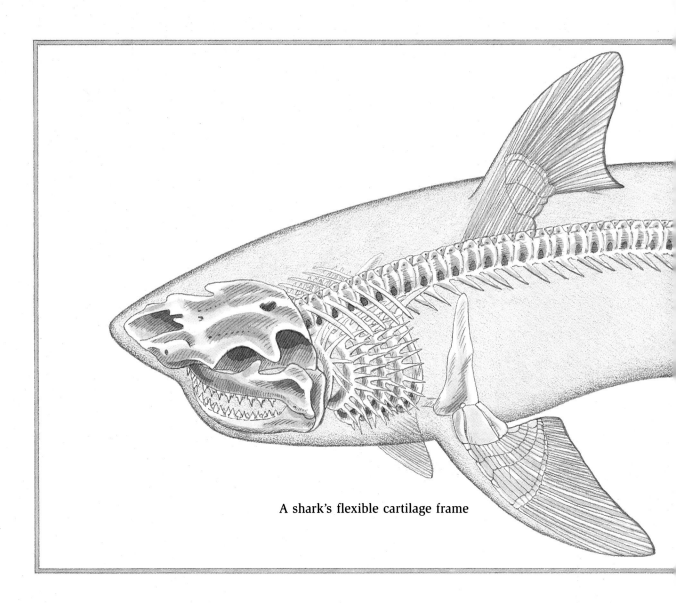

A shark's flexible cartilage frame

Even though sharks can be so different from one another, they are alike in other ways. All sharks are fish, live in water, and have lots of teeth. But they are very unusual fish. While other fish have bony skeletons, all sharks have a softer frame made of cartilage, just like the tip of your nose.

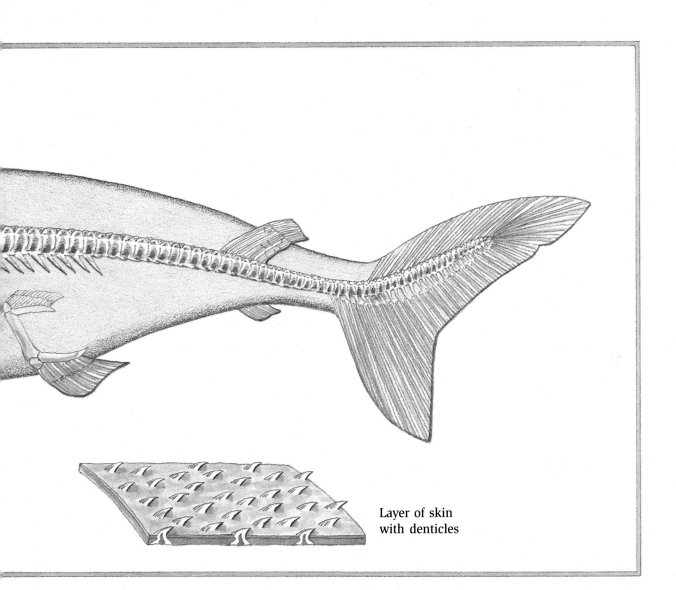

Layer of skin
with denticles

The bodies of sharks are covered with denticles, or small tooth-like spikes, instead of the scales that other fish have.

While other fish can stay afloat without swimming, sharks must swim constantly or they will sink. They cannot stop suddenly or swim backwards like other fish. Sharks must swerve to the side to avoid hitting something in their path.

All sharks have an amazing system of senses. They have the ability to feel everything that happens in the water around them. This makes it very easy for sharks to find food.
A large part of a shark's brain is used for the sense of smell. Sharks are aware of the tiniest trace of an odor, even from a great distance.

Nurse Shark

Scientists used to think that sharks did not see very well. But now it is known that most sharks have excellent vision, particularly close up.

Sharks also have great hearing. In addition, they have special body parts that allow them to feel vibrations or movement far away in the water. They can even sense electricity given off by other living things.

It is not easy to study sharks. In the wild, it can be dangerous to get close to them. Sharks are strong and powerful in the water, but are extremely delicate when lifted up out of the water. They can easily be injured, and it is hard to keep them alive. No one is sure just why, but many kinds of sharks do not live very long in captivity.

Still, over the years, animal researchers have learned many interesting facts about sharks. For instance, it used to be thought that sharks were always hungry and always hunting for food. But now, it is known that sharks sometimes go for long periods, even up to a month, without eating.

Blue Sharks

| Great White Shark | Tiger Shark | Mako Shark | Lemon Shark | Bull Shark |

Everyone knows that sharks have many teeth, but most people don't know just how many teeth sharks can have. Sharks have many sets of teeth in their mouths at one time and any time they lose a tooth, a new one replaces it. In its lifetime, a shark can go through thousands of teeth!

The mouth of a swellshark, close up

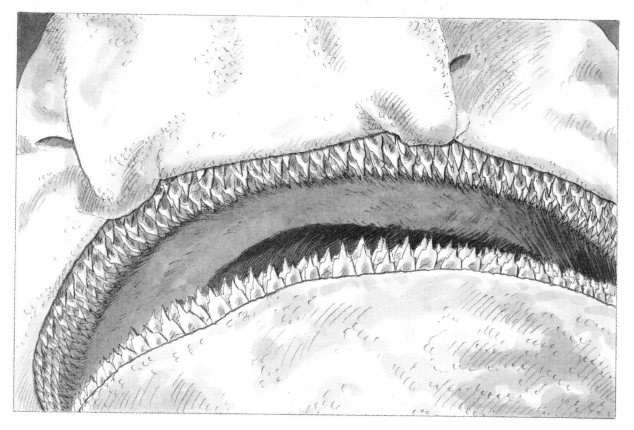

Certain sharks are particularly interesting to scientists. The bull shark is unusual because it can live in the ocean *and* in freshwater lakes and rivers! All other sharks must stay in salt water. Another shark, the megamouth, was never seen until quite recently. No one even knew it existed. Only a few have been sighted so far.

Megamouth

A swellshark baby develops in an
egg case attached to seaweed

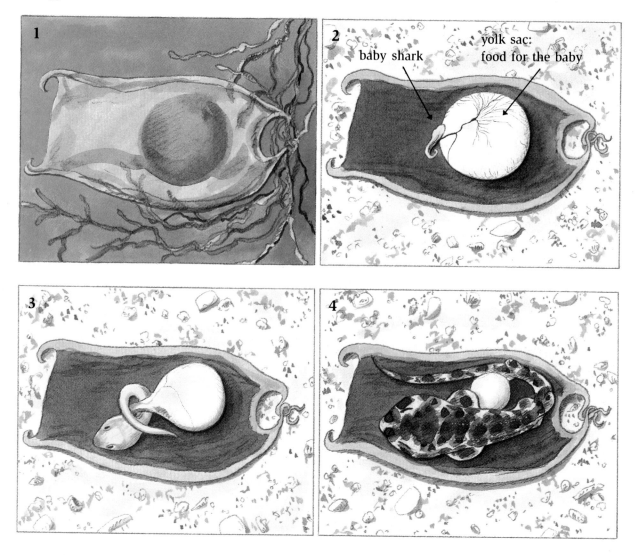

1

2 baby shark   yolk sac:
                food for the baby

3

4

In studying sharks, much has been learned about the way baby sharks are born. Some hatch from eggs outside the mother's body.

Most sharks are born live, like mammals. Some sharks can have as many as 100 babies at a time! Other sharks have as few as two.

Baby sharks can take care of themselves as soon as they are born and can already give quite a bite! Since sharks do sometimes eat other sharks, it is a very good thing that a mother shark stops feeding when it is time to give birth. Otherwise, she would probably eat all her babies!

Lemon shark pups
are born live

The fact that sharks do eat other sharks is the reason for this amazing story: a man once caught four sharks all at the same time!

Tiger Shark

Bull Shark

He pulled in a tiger shark. In its stomach was a bull shark.
Inside the bull shark's stomach was a blacktip shark, and
inside *it* was a small dogfish shark!

Blacktip Shark

Dogfish

Each year, thousands of sharks are killed by people. They are killed for food, oil, skins, and sport. But only a very small number of people are actually killed each year by sharks. Usually, a shark attacks a person only in its natural search for food. Sharks are dangerous because they are large, wild animals with big teeth, looking for a meal. It is not because sharks are bad or evil.

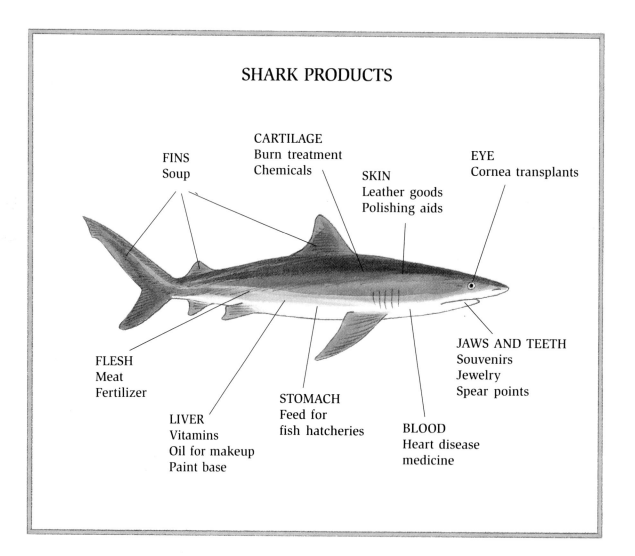

SHARK PRODUCTS

FINS
Soup

CARTILAGE
Burn treatment
Chemicals

SKIN
Leather goods
Polishing aids

EYE
Cornea transplants

FLESH
Meat
Fertilizer

LIVER
Vitamins
Oil for makeup
Paint base

STOMACH
Feed for
fish hatcheries

BLOOD
Heart disease
medicine

JAWS AND TEETH
Souvenirs
Jewelry
Spear points

Sharks are no more dangerous than other large wild animals such as lions and tigers. The water is the natural home of the shark. When people enter the water, they may very well meet up with a shark.

Both sharks and people are important links in the chain of living things on this planet. People must share the earth with many living things, including sharks. The more we learn about sharks, the safer we will be, and the safer sharks will be.

The awesome shark deserves to be respected and admired as well as feared. We still have so much to learn about this fascinating fish!

Hammerhead Shark

MORE ABOUT SHARKS

The 350 species of sharks are divided into 8 large orders or groups. These are divided into smaller groups of 30 families. Some of these families include dogfish sharks, sawsharks, angelsharks, carpetsharks (including whale, zebra, and nurse sharks), bullhead sharks, sand tigers, basking sharks, goblin sharks, threshers, catsharks, and requiem sharks.

Members of the same family not only look alike but behave in a similar way. They live in the same kinds of places. The area where a particular family of sharks lives depends on both the temperature of the water and how deep it is. Each group of sharks has a temperature and depth it prefers. Every shark has specialized body parts for the particular way it lives.

Sharks must always be moving to keep afloat. Other fish have balloon-like sacs inside them, called swim bladders, that fill with air or gas and keep them afloat. Sharks do not have swim bladders and will sink if they stop moving.

A shark's liver is very large and takes up about one quarter of its total body weight. The liver contains oil, which is lighter than water. The more a shark eats, the more oil there is in its liver. The shark becomes lighter in the water and it is easier to stay afloat. When a shark has not eaten for a while, it becomes heavier in the water, making it more difficult to stay afloat. It is hard to lift sharks up out of the water because sharks are so heavy, and they weigh even more in the air than they do in the water.

Sharks have special body parts called lateral lines on the sides of their bodies. These parts are very sensitive to vibrations in the water. Sharks have groups of tiny holes in their faces that can pick up the electrical signals given off by other living things in the water. This system of holes is called the *Ampullae of Lorenzini*. Their unusual body equipment, keen hearing and sense of smell make sharks excellent hunters.

Sharks caught commercially are used for many things. Their meat is eaten or used for fertilizer. Their oils are used for vitamins, lubricants, and cosmetics. Shark teeth and jaws have been used for centuries to make jewelry and primitive weapons. Shark skins are used for making leather goods. Their eyes, blood, and cartilage are often used in medical treatment and research.